WORLD CLASS CITIES

# Sydney

Heather Kissock

AV2
www.av2books.com

**Step 1**
Go to **www.av2books.com**

**Step 2**
Enter this unique code

**TDHLJU5NA**

**Step 3**
Explore your interactive eBook!

AV2 is optimized for use on any device

# Your interactive eBook comes with...

**Contents**
Browse a live contents page to easily navigate through resources

**Audio**
Listen to sections of the book read aloud

**Videos**
Watch informative video clips

**Weblinks**
Gain additional information for research

**Try This!**
Complete activities and hands-on experiments

**Key Words**
Study vocabulary, and complete a matching word activity

**Quizzes**
Test your knowledge

**Slideshows**
View images and captions

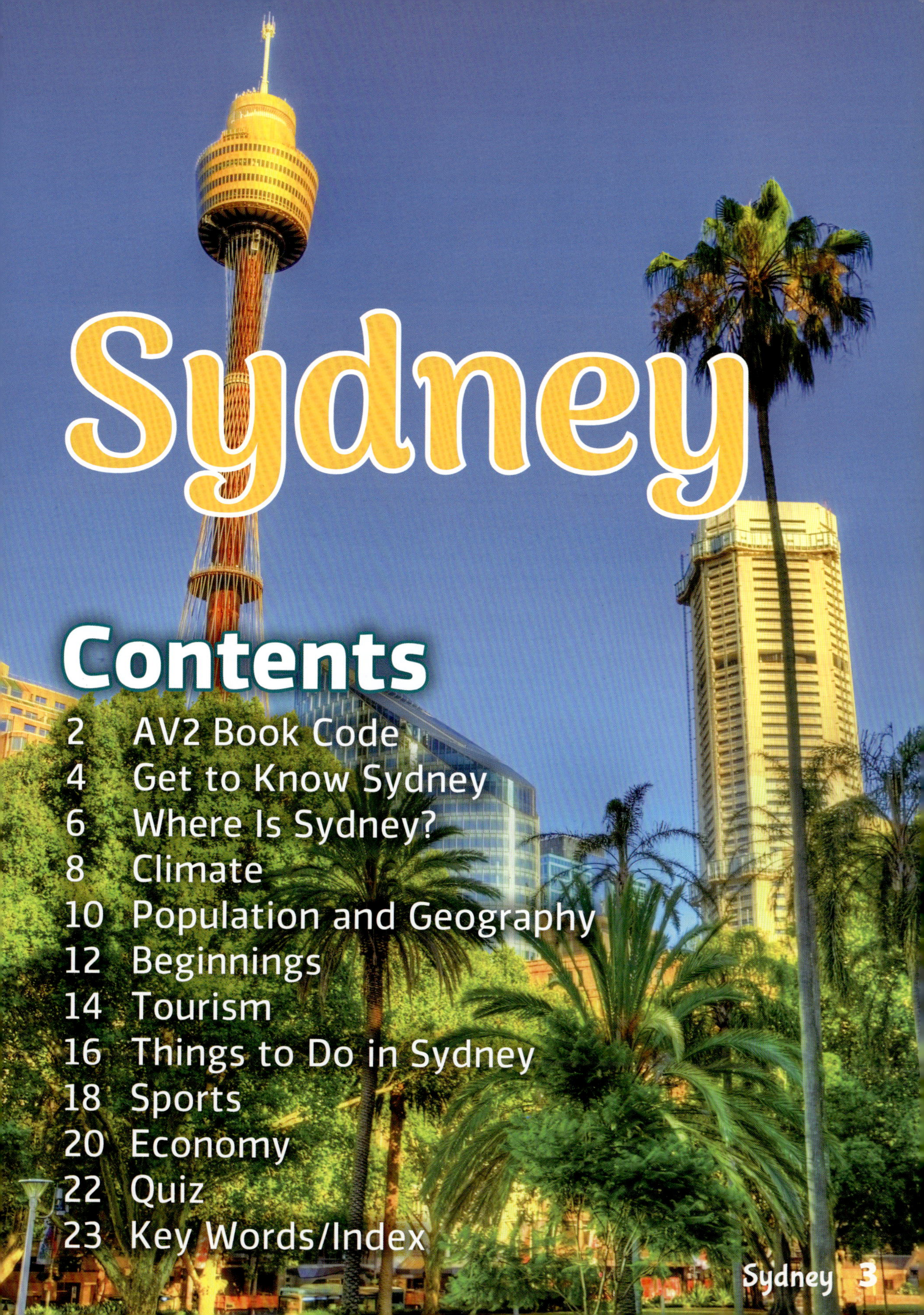

# Sydney

## Contents


2 AV2 Book Code
4 Get to Know Sydney
6 Where Is Sydney?
8 Climate
10 Population and Geography
12 Beginnings
14 Tourism
16 Things to Do in Sydney
18 Sports
20 Economy
22 Quiz
23 Key Words/Index

# Get to Know Sydney

## Comparing World Bridges

Tower Bridge (United Kingdom)
800 feet long
(244 meters)

Sydney Harbour Bridge (Australia)
3,770 feet long
(1,149m)

Golden Gate Bridge (United States)
8,981 feet long
(2,737 m)

Akashi Strait Bridge (Japan)
12,831 feet long
(3,911 m)

Sydney is the largest city in Australia. It is also the capital of a state called New South Wales. The city is known for its scenic **harbor**. Sydney's Harbour Bridge stretches across the harbor. It links the northern and southern parts of the city.

# Where Is Sydney?

Sydney sits on Australia's southeast coast. Australia is both a country and a **continent**. It is also an island. Two oceans surround it. These are the Pacific and Indian Oceans.

There are many places to visit in Australia. Some people come to see the Outback. This desert covers much of Australia. Others want to learn about the continent's **Indigenous Peoples**. Australia's unique animals also bring visitors from around the world.

## Words to Know

People in Australia speak English,
but some of their words are specific to them.

# Climate

Sydney is known for its mild **climate**. Summers are warm and sunny. Winters are cool. Most of the city's rain falls between March and May. This is the city's fall season.

Desert winds can bring dry, hot air to the Sydney area. This sometimes causes forest fires just outside the city. Smoke can fill the air.

## A Year in Sydney

**Average Summer Temperature**
77° Fahrenheit (25° Celsius)

**Average Winter Temperature**
56° Fahrenheit (13°C)

**Average Annual Rainfall**
47 inches (1,200 millimeters)

SHANGRI-LA HOTEL
QUAY WEST
END RESTRICTED PARKING AREA
THE ROCKS

# Population and Geography

Sydney is home to about 5 million people. The population of Australia as a whole is more than 25 million. This means about one in five Australians lives in Sydney.

Downtown Sydney sits along the shores of **Port** Jackson. This is another name for Sydney Harbour. Port Jackson stretches 12 miles (19 km) into the city. Several islands dot its waters.

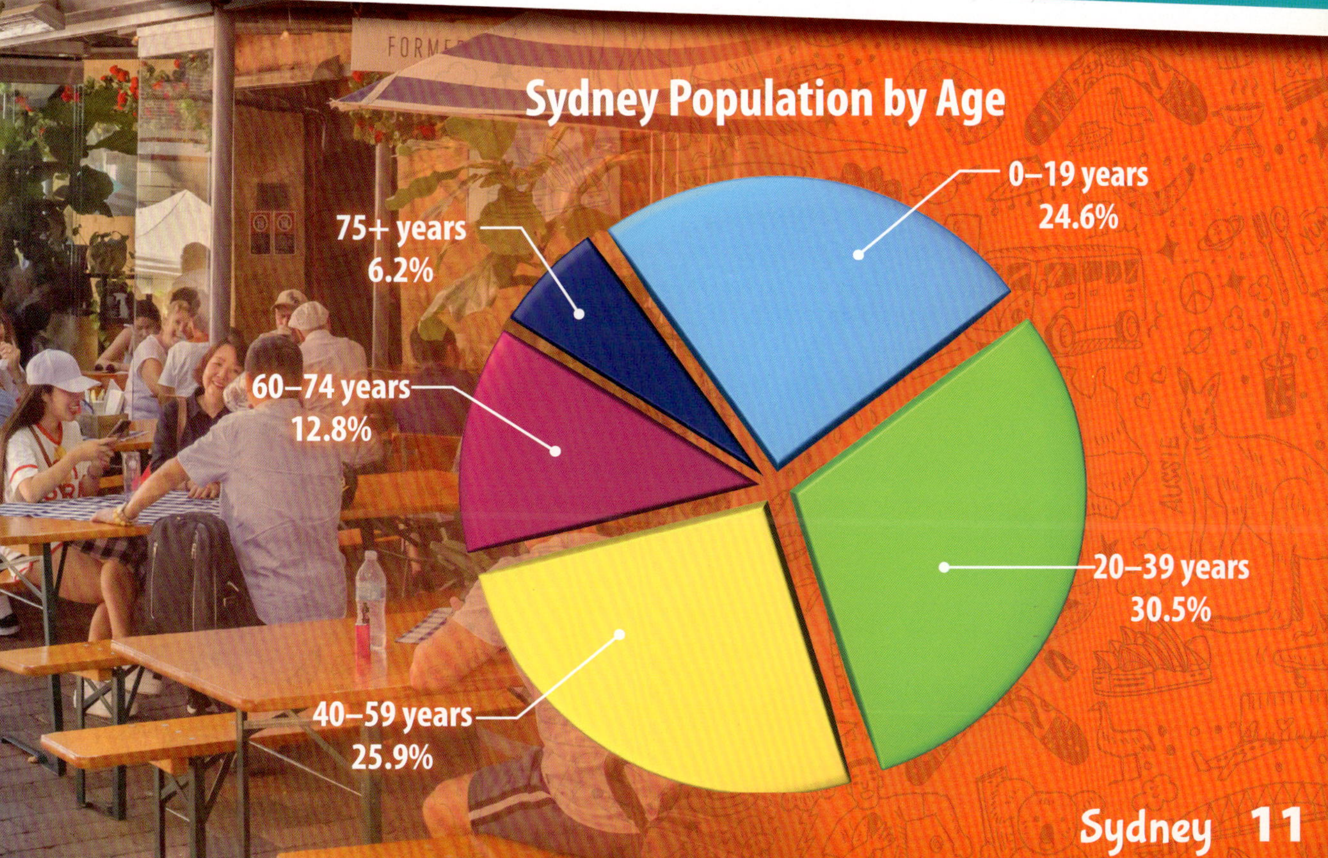

# Beginnings

Indigenous Peoples lived in what is now Sydney long before anyone else. The English first explored the area in 1700s. They set up a **colony** there. Many of the first Europeans to arrive were convicts. These are people who have broken the law.

Over time, other **settlers** arrived. Soon, people from all over the world began moving to Sydney. Today, people from many countries live in the city.

## Sydney Timeline

Sydney has been the site of many important events over the years. All have made the city what it is today.

**45,000 years ago**

Indigenous Peoples live in and around the area now called Sydney.

**1770 AD**

England's James Cook explores the coast along what is now Sydney.

**1788**

The first European settlers arrive and set up a colony.

1842

Sydney becomes a city.

1932

The Sydney Harbour Bridge opens.

2019

Sydney's landmarks are hidden from view when smoke from forest fires covers the city.

## Tourism

Most visitors to Sydney spend time at the harbor. Some climb to the top of the Harbour Bridge. Others go to a show at the Sydney Opera House. Boat tours of the harbor are also popular.

Sydney Tower offers visitors great views of the city. The tower is the city's tallest building. It rises to a height of 1,014 feet (309 meters).

# Things to Do in Sydney

## Bondi Beach

These white sands make up Australia's most visited beach. People from all over the world come here to surf and sunbathe.

## The Rocks

This is the oldest part of Sydney. Today, people walk the **cobblestone** streets to visit its shops and restaurants.

## Taronga Zoo

This zoo overlooks Sydney Harbour. It is home to more than 5,000 animals.

## Sea Life Sydney

Stingrays, sea turtles, dugongs, and more can all be found at this aquarium. Visitors can even snorkel with the aquarium's sharks.

## Australian National Maritime Museum

Visitors come to this museum to learn more about life at sea. Its attractions include an 18th century **tall ship** and a naval submarine.

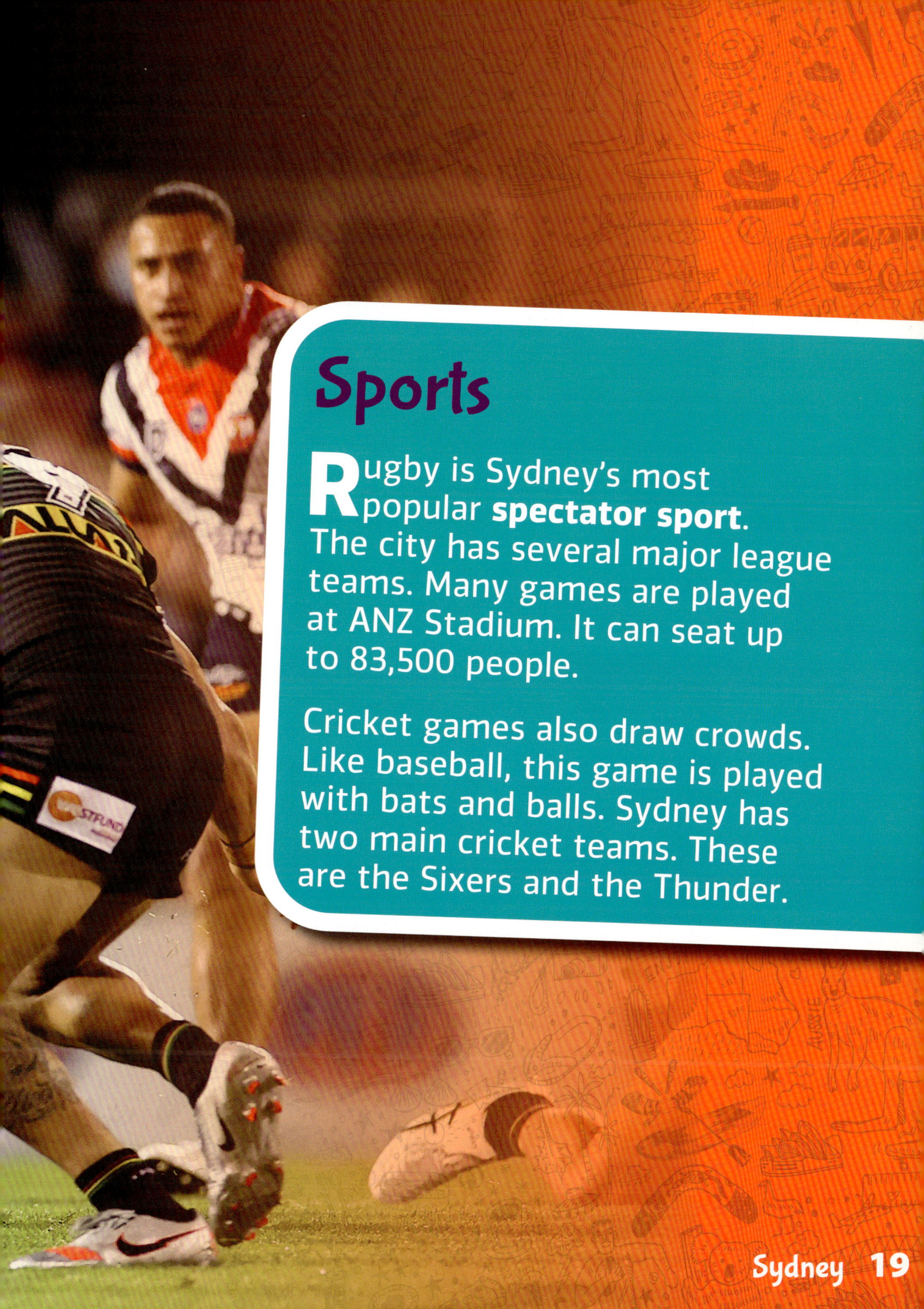

# Sports

Rugby is Sydney's most popular **spectator sport**. The city has several major league teams. Many games are played at ANZ Stadium. It can seat up to 83,500 people.

Cricket games also draw crowds. Like baseball, this game is played with bats and balls. Sydney has two main cricket teams. These are the Sixers and the Thunder.

# Economy

Sydney is the key business center for Australia. Many banks and other companies have their main offices in the city. Most of these companies are located in the Central Business District, or CBD.

Sydney is also a center for **trade**. The city is home to one of Australia's largest ports. Every day, ships arrive at Port Botany with **goods** to sell. The ships also take goods made in Australia to other countries.

COSCO FELIXSTOWE

# Quiz

**1** Which Australian state is Sydney the capital of?

**ANSWER:** New South Wales

**2** When does Sydney's fall season take place?

**ANSWER:** Between March and May

**3** How many people live in Sydney?

**ANSWER:** About 5 million

**4** When did the first European settlers arrive and set up a colony in what is now Sydney?

**ANSWER:** 1788

**5** What is the name of Sydney's tallest building?

**ANSWER:** Sydney Tower

**6** What is the oldest part of Sydney called?

**ANSWER:** The Rocks

**7** What is Sydney's most popular spectator sport?

**ANSWER:** Rugby

**8** What part of Sydney is home to the main offices of banks and other companies?

**ANSWER:** The Central Business District, or CBD

# Key Words

**climate:** the average weather conditions of a region throughout a year

**cobblestone:** a round stone once used to pave streets

**colony:** a territory ruled by another country

**continent:** one of seven large land areas on Earth

**goods:** things that are sold

**harbor:** a sheltered place along a coast

**Indigenous Peoples:** groups of people that are native to a certain place

**port:** a place where boats can dock safely

**settlers:** people who move to a new land and make it their home

**spectator sport:** a sport that people go to watch

**tall ship:** a sailing boat with high masts

**trade:** the business of buying and selling goods

# Index


Australia 4, 5, 6, 7, 11, 16, 20
Australian National Maritime Museum 17

Bondi Beach 16

Central Business District (CBD) 20, 22
climate 8
colony 12, 22
Cook, James 12
cricket 19

forest fires 8, 13

harbor 5, 11, 14, 17

Indigenous Peoples 7, 12

New South Wales 5, 22

Port Botany 20
Port Jackson 11

rugby 19, 22

Sea Life Sydney 17
Sydney Harbour 5, 11, 17
Sydney Harbour Bridge 4, 5, 13, 14
Sydney Opera House 14, 15
Sydney Tower 14, 22

Taronga Zoo 17
The Rocks 16, 22

# Get the best of both worlds.

AV2 bridges the gap between print and digital.

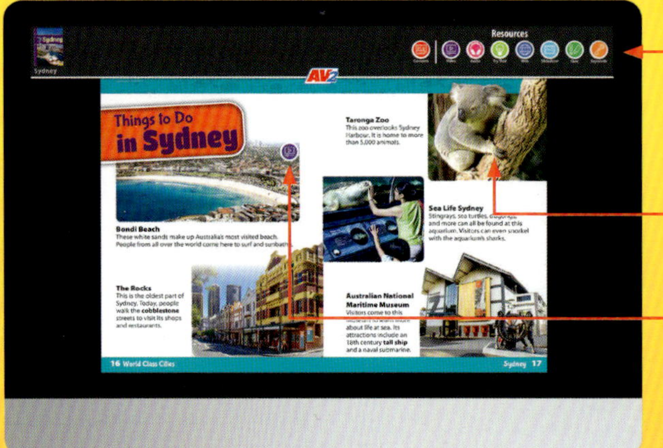

The expandable resources toolbar enables quick access to content including **videos**, **audio**, **activities**, **weblinks**, **slideshows**, **quizzes**, and **key words**.

**Animated videos** make static images come alive.

Resource icons on each page help readers to further **explore key concepts**.

Published by AV2
276 5th Avenue, Suite 704 #917
New York, NY 10001
Website: www.av2books.com



Library of Congress Cataloging-in-Publication Data
Names: Kissock, Heather, author.
Title: Sydney / Heather Kissock.
Description: New York : AV2, 2022. | Series: World class cities | Includes index. | Audience: Ages 8-11 | Audience: Grades 2-3
Identifiers: LCCN 2021003455 (print) | LCCN 2021003456 (ebook) | ISBN 9781791138424 (library binding) | ISBN 9781791138431 (paperback) | ISBN 9781791138448
Subjects: LCSH: Sydney (N.S.W.)--Juvenile literature.
Classification: LCC DU178 .K56 2022 (print) | LCC DU178 (ebook) | DDC 944.4/1--dc23
LC record available at https://lccn.loc.gov/2021003455
LC ebook record available at https://lccn.loc.gov/2021003456

Printed in Guangzhou, China
1 2 3 4 5 6 7 8 9 0 25 24 23 22 21

022021
101120

Project Coordinator: Heather Kissock
Designer: Ana María Vidal

Every reasonable effort has been made to trace ownership and to obtain permission to reprint copyright material. The publishers would be pleased to have any errors or omissions brought to their attention so that they may be corrected in subsequent printings.

AV2 acknowledges Getty Images, Alamy, and Dreamstime as its primary image suppliers for this title.